Dietitian
IN THE
KITCHEN

Dietitian in the Kitchen™

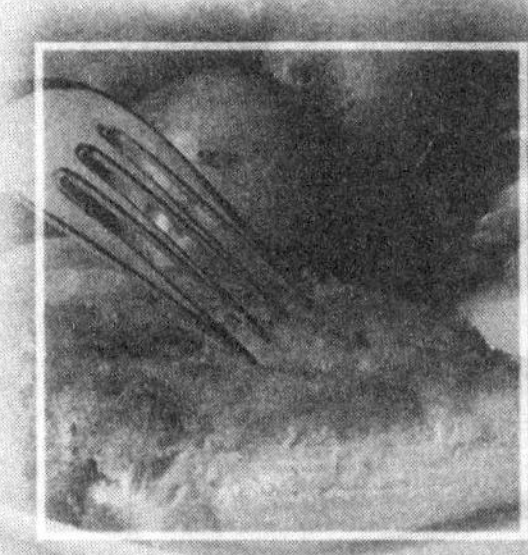

Volume I: The Essential Recipes

Diane M. Henderiks, R.D.

Editor	Diane M. Henderiks, R.D.
Associate Editor	Cindy Nixon
Art Direction	Jimmy Bliziotis
Design & Production	Alice Heinzelman
Printing	Prototype Marketing & Design, Inc.

ISBN Number 0-9772907-051995 (paperbound)

First Edition, 2005.

Printed in the United States of America.

Volume I:

The Essential Recipes

Diane M. Henderiks, R.D.

Registered Dietitian

Dedication

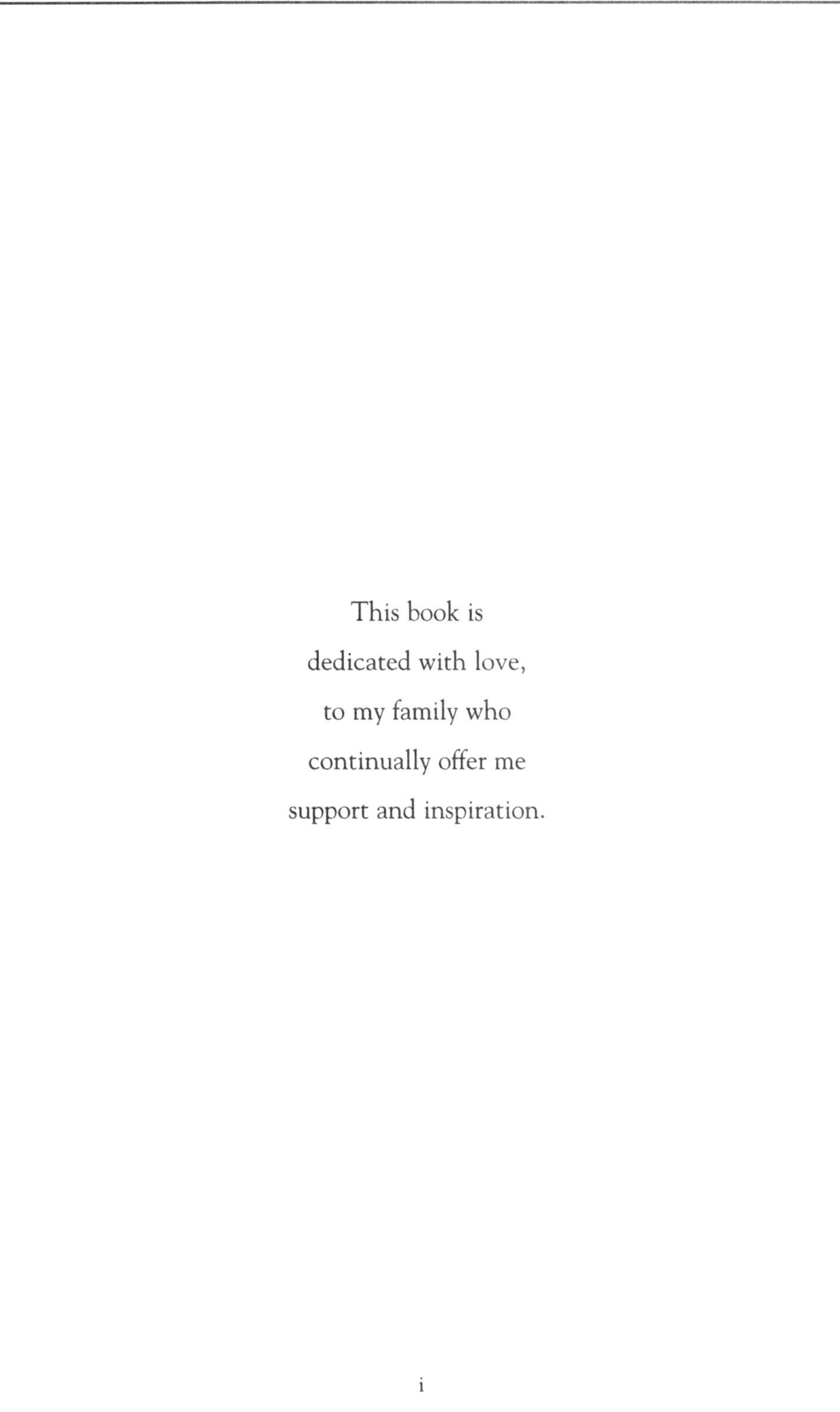

This book is
dedicated with love,
to my family who
continually offer me
support and inspiration.

Acknowledgements

As a Registered Dietitian I obviously think about the kinds of foods people eat, and the resulting health issues in our culture today. There is a need for information! When people are informed about the ways in which food affects their lives, they can make the right choices when it comes cooking, nutrition, food and a healthful lifestyle. Combining my nutrition expertise and my passion for cooking has been a natural progression and a way to share the knowledge I have gained over the years. There are many people who have been an inspiration for this book series.

I must first express gratitude to my husband, Erick, who has given unconditional support to this endeavor. He has spent countless days and evenings watching our two beautiful boys while I was either cooking or writing. He has been my taste tester, critic and biggest fan. This book would not have been possible without him. I love you, Erick!

My parents, Ralph and Nöel Cannito, my sisters Laura and Alison and all of the other family members and friends who have sampled most of the recipes featured in this book and have given me both love and encouragement.

My marketing director and friend, Jimmy Bliziotis who's marketing genius has been an incredible asset to the growth of my nutrition practice. Jimmy has facilitated the creation of this book series and has been by my side from the beginning.

Lastly, I wish to thank my sons, Lukas and Derek, who are a constant source of joy in my life!

Contents

Introduction

Most of us take for granted the best things in life. Think about it: You just trust that your car will run in the morning, getting you where you need to go. You just assume that the computer will start up at work, the call to your best friend will be connected, the birthday card delivered to your grandmother on time. Every fall, we just expect to see the brilliant hues of changing leaves outside our windows; and every winter, we nonchalantly imprint our footsteps on the pristine snow. Most of all, we just figure our loved ones will always be there for us, just as we will be for them, right?

Health is one of those things that a lot of us take for granted an awful lot of the time. We assume we're entitled to it, and we therefore don't give it much thought. Until something goes wrong, that is. Then we see that health is not only one of the best things in life, it's perhaps the best thing in life. Then we understand all those toasts to our health at special occasions, all those doctor's orders we didn't quite follow, all those mother's warnings we didn't fully heed.

But, fortunately, good health is something we can create. It's not as random and mysterious as why a computer suddenly crashes (well, that's a mystery to most of us, at least), nor is it beyond our control, as is the miraculous changing of the seasons each year. On the contrary, good health is the direct result of choices we make on a daily basis and, for the most part, it is an utterly controllable element in our lives. And two of the best ways to both control and create good health are to (1) consume healthy foods and (2) participate in an adequate amount of physical activity — in other words, that commonsensical recipe for success: diet and exercise. But by "diet," I don't mean depriving yourself of taste and depleting your culinary enjoyment. I don't mean fasting or taking supplements or turning everything you eat into a smoothie. No. I mean, quite simply, healthy eating. I mean trusting that your body knows what's good for it and fueling it with the energy it desires to produce fantastic results.

To attain these results, you need only feast upon meals that are both delicious and nutritious. Preparing such meals, I know, may seem like a daunting task to the uninitiated cook, but it really doesn't have to be. The truth is, all of the ingredients required to prepare healthy meals are easy to obtain and easy to work with. All you need to do to cook healthy is keep a well-stocked pantry and fridge filled with the kind of good-quality ingredients you'll find on the shopping list included in this book.

With these items on hand, you can prepare better meals faster and, in the process, progress faster toward a healthy state. That's what this book series is for — to introduce you to the basics of healthy eating, to detail just what and how much you should be eating to both achieve and maintain health, to provide pointers and tips that will facilitate this transformation, and to offer a slew of recipes that will put your newfound knowledge to work for you and for everyone who dines at your table.

The real key to healthy eating is to select items that are as close to their natural state as possible, which necessarily means selecting a minimal amount of processed foods (if any at all). For example, choose fresh fruits and vegetables over canned varieties; whole grains like barley and bulgur wheat over refined white flour; couscous and wild or brown rice over white rice and pastas; and sweet potatoes not just white potatoes. For protein staples, choose lean, skinless and boneless poultry and fish, as well as the leaner cuts of red meat, such as filet mignon, sirloin and round steaks. And, of course, never underestimate the extreme benefits of such soy-based products as tofu and tempeh. This theory applies to all parts of your diet, both large and small. So rather than snack upon or garnish foods with fried tidbits or refined bread products, try raw nuts and seeds. Instead of flavoring your food with excess salt and fat, select spices that will enhance natural flavors and add zest to your dishes without adding extra calories and unhealthy byproducts.

Don't worry. You don't have to decide what to buy, how to prepare it, and what seasonings to use on your own. That's what you will find in the pages of this book. And the first step is to inspect your kitchen to see what food items you can get rid of and replace with healthier choices. Good-bye processed yellow cheese slices, hello low-fat mozzarella. Au revoir canned soup, bonjour homemade stocks rife with tender veggies. Exit frosted flakes, enter shredded wheat.

This recipe book will then help you shop for and prepare meals that are short on fat, sodium and simple sugars, yet long on flavor. The recipes can certainly be used by people who have conditions such as diabetes, high cholesterol or hypertension and those looking to manage their weight. But you should know that this isn't a medical cookbook. Nevertheless, because the quality of the foods used and the nutritional value of the recipes are so high, the meals are appropriate for nearly everyone.

And because so many medical conditions are impacted by excess weight, portion control is a major focus of this approach to healthy eating, whether or not you have some medical ailment or have some extra weight you want to lose. So quantity is indeed as important as quality, and this concept is put into effect here by consuming one serving of whatever dish you've prepared and then balancing out the rest of your plate with an assortment of other wholesome foods, those too in the proper serving sizes.

If you follow these guidelines, you'll adopt the sort of "non-dieting" approach to eating I endorse, one that doesn't rely on weighing or measuring ingredients or dissecting food labels. Even if you don't have a medical condition or a weight problem, then, you'll be eating like you do, for — and here's the crucial point — all of us should indeed be eating to avoid such problems all the time, regardless of whether we already have them and are looking to reverse them or whether we're just trying to prevent them in the first place. That's what healthy eating is. That's where this book will lead you. As long as your choices include a variety of healthful foods consumed in moderation, you will achieve nutritional health. You'll learn to use your permanent knowledge to make intelligent food choices rather than letting your temporary hunger and fleeting cravings dictate your eating habits. It's about lifestyle changes, not restrictive diets. It's about controlling what you can to create what you want. It's all about health. Don't take it for granted for one more day of your life. Honor your health now by honoring what your body naturally knows and what it was ultimately made for.

It's all about LIFESTYLE CHANGES not diets!!"

CULINARY

CONVERSIONS

Weight Conversions:

1 pound	16 ounces = 454 grams
1 ounce	28.35 grams
1 kilogram	1000 grams = 2.2 pounds
1 gram	1000 milligrams
1 milligram	1000 micrograms
1 microgram	0.001 milligrams

Volume Conversions:

1 gallon	128 fluid ounces = 16 cups = 8 pints = 4 quarts = 3.79 liters
1 quart	32 fluid ounces = 4 cups = 2 pints = 946.36 milliliters
1 pint	16 fluid ounces = 2 cups
1 cup	8 fluid ounces = 1/2 pint = 16 tablespoons = 237 milliliters
1/3 cup	16 teaspoons = 5 tablespoons + 1 teaspoon
1 fluid ounce	1/8 cup = 2 tablespoons = 29.6 milliliter
1 tablespoon	1/2 fluid ounce = 3 teaspoons = 1/16 cup = 14.79 milliliters
1 teaspoon	1/3 tablespoon = 4.93 milliliters = approx. 5 grams dry weight
1 liter	1.06 quart = 1000 milliliters
1 milliliter	0.03 fluid ounce

Healthy Substitutions

Many of us choose far too many foods that are high in fat, salt and sugar. It is simple to improve the nutritional value of recipes without sacrificing flavor. The first step is to identify unhealthy ingredients and decide whether you can…

1. Get rid of it! If you don't need it….don't use it!

2. Cut down on it! Less is at most times best….especially when it comes to fat, salt and sugar!

3. Replace it! Experiment with healthier ingredients!

Use the following list to make healthy substitutions

INSTEAD OF...	TRY...
Butter, Lard, & other Saturated Fat (Coconut Oil, Palm Oil)	*Soft tub margarine (trans-fat free & non hydrogenated. The first ingredient on food label should be liquid vegetable oil)* *Broth* *Olive or canola oil*
Whole Milk	*Skim. 1 percent milk, soy milk*
Cream	*Evaporated skim milk*
Sour Cream	*Plain low-fat yogurt* *1/2 cup. cottage cheese blended with 1 & 1/2 teaspoon. Lemon juice* *Low-fat sour cream*
Cream Soup	*Broth-based or skim milk-based soups*
Full-fat Cheese	*Low-fat, skim-milk cheese* *Cheese with less than 3 grams of fat per ounce* *Soy cheese*
Whipped Cream	*Chilled, whipped evaporated skim milk* *Non-dairy whipped topping made from polyunsaturated fat*
Ice Cream	*Low-fat or non-fat ice cream* *Frozen low-fat or non-fat yogurt* *Frozen fruit juice products* *Sorbet* *(All in no more than 1/2 cup portions)*

INSTEAD OF...	TRY...
Mayonnaise	*Low-fat mayonnaise* *Plain low-fat yogurt combined with low-fat cottage cheese* *Mustard*
Salad Dressing	*Homemade dressing made with unsaturated oils, water, various vinegars, garlic, lemon juice & spices*
Whole Egg	*Two egg whites* *1/4 cup. cholesterol-free liquid egg product* *Liquid egg whites*
Ground Beef	*Ground sirloin* *Lean ground turkey or chicken breast*
Sausage or Bacon	*Turkey, chicken or soy sausage* *Turkey, chicken or soy bacon* *Canadian bacon* *Lean ham*
White Rice & Pasta	*Brown rice, bulgur, quinoa, whole wheat pasta, any whole grain*
Salt	*Fresh & dried herbs, hot & black pepper*

Are you confused at the supermarket? It is no wonder, as the average supermarket has over 30,000 items and not every supermarket has the same 30,000! In 1900, Americans chose from among 500 or so different foods; today we choose from more than 50,000. These figures help explain why it is difficult to make healthy choices at the supermarket because temptation is everywhere. Foods come in a wide variety of forms – however those items that are part of a nutritious diet consist of low-fat dairy, lean meat/poultry/fish, soy, vegetables, legumes, fruits and whole grains. You must have these ingredients on hand to cook healthy!

Go through your cabinets and refrigerator before you venture to the supermarket. This way you can see what you have on hand and what you need to buy. Then make a list! Although it may take a little longer to shop at first, the benefits will be worthwhile. A list is very important because it will help you to:

- Make healthier choices
- Reduce impulse buying
- Save money because you are not grabbing foods that are not on the list
- Spend less time at the supermarket
- Become an educated consumer

The periphery of the grocery store has most of the healthiest choices; produce, lean meat/poultry/fish, low-fat dairy and whole grain breads. Don't stop there, you will find other nutritious foods in the middle aisles also like whole grains, beans, unsweetened cereals, soy products, water and flavored seltzers.

Many people purchase a lot of pre-packaged foods for convenience. Some choices are much better than others. Look for foods that have the least amount of fat, sugar and sodium. Read the labels so you can make the best choices. Choose convenience foods in moderation and as I mentioned before freshly prepared meals are always the best!

HERE ARE SOME OF THE TERMS YOU MIGHT SEE WHILE YOU ARE SHOPPING:

- Healthy - the food is low in fat (especially saturated fat or trans fat, which has been linked to heart disease) and has limited amounts of cholesterol and sodium.
- Free (for example, sugar free) - the food contains only tiny amounts of fat, saturated fat, sodium, sugar, cholesterol, or calories per serving.
- Good source - one serving provides 10% to 19% of your total daily needs for a specific nutrient.
- Low-sodium - one serving has 140 milligrams of sodium or less.
- Low cholesterol - one serving has 20 milligrams of cholesterol or less and 2 grams or less of saturated fat.
- Low-fat - one serving contains 3 grams of fat or less.
- Reduced (for example, reduced fat) - one serving has 25% less fat, saturated fat, sodium, sugar, cholesterol, or calories per serving than the regular version of the food.
- Light (or lite) - one serving has 50% less fat or one third fewer calories than the regular version of the food.

DIETITIAN in the KITCHEN™

RULE:

If it's not on the list…don't buy it!
There is no need for added temptation staring
you in the face at home.

The following 7 guidelines will help
you to be a health smart grocery shopper!

1. NEVER go grocery shopping hungry!
2. Choose the SMALLEST fruits and veggies!
   ("Nature packs many of our fruits and veggies in perfect serving sizes")
3. Choose LEAN meats, poultry and fish!
4. Choose LOW-FAT dairy products!
5. Choose WHOLE GRAIN breads and cereals… avoid refined products!
6. Opt for LOW-SODIUM products whenever available!
7. Let your INTELLIGENCE make your food choices NOT momentary, fleeting cravings!

Shopping List

Use the following shopping list to be certain that your grocery cart is filled with delicious and nutritious foods!

Veggies

- ❏ Arugula
- ❏ Asparagus
- ❏ Avocado
- ❏ Broccoli
- ❏ Brussels Sprouts
- ❏ Cabbage
- ❏ Carrots
- ❏ Cauliflower
- ❏ Celery
- ❏ Cucumbers
- ❏ Eggplant
- ❏ Fennel
- ❏ Fresh Herbs
- ❏ Garlic
- ❏ Green Beans
- ❏ Jicama
- ❏ Leafy Greens (Lettuce, Kale, Collards...)
- ❏ Mushrooms
- ❏ Onions
- ❏ Peppers
- ❏ Potatoes
- ❏ Radishes
- ❏ Spinach
- ❏ Sweet Potatoes
- ❏ Tomatoes
- ❏ Zucchini

Fruits

- ❏ Apples
- ❏ Bananas
- ❏ Berries
- ❏ Cherries
- ❏ Grapes
- ❏ Grapefruit
- ❏ Kiwi
- ❏ Lemons
- ❏ Limes
- ❏ Mangos
- ❏ Melon
- ❏ Oranges
- ❏ Papaya
- ❏ Peaches
- ❏ Pears
- ❏ Pineapple
- ❏ Strawberries
- ❏ Tangerines

Groceries

- ❑ Anchovies
- ❑ Canned Pumpkin
- ❑ Dijon Mustard
- ❑ Dried Beans
- ❑ Dried Herbs/Spices
- ❑ Dried Unsweetened Fruit
- ❑ Evaporated Skim Milk
- ❑ Extra Virgin Olive Oil
- ❑ Flavored Vinegars
- ❑ Hot Sauces
- ❑ Ketchup
- ❑ Kosher Salt/Peppercorns
- ❑ Lite Soy/Lite Teriyaki
- ❑ Low-Sodium Broth
- ❑ Low-Sodium Canned Tomatoes
- ❑ Low-Fat Mayo
- ❑ Olives
- ❑ Balsamic, Rice & Red Wine Vinegar
- ❑ Salsa
- ❑ Sesame & Peanut Oil
- ❑ Tuna In Water
- ❑ Popcorn Kernels
- ❑ Rice Cakes
- ❑ Soy Crisps

Deli

(Low-Fat/Low-Sodium <3g Fat/Oz.)

- ❑ Turkey
- ❑ Roast Beef
- ❑ Ham

Desserts

(Consume 1 Serving)

- ❑ 100% Frozen Fruit Bars
- ❑ Fig Newtons
- ❑ Gingersnaps
- ❑ Graham Crackers
- ❑ Low-fat Frozen Yogurt
- ❑ Low-fat Pudding Cups

Beverages

- ❑ Seltzer
- ❑ Flavored Seltzer
- ❑ Low-Sodium V8
- ❑ Green Tea
- ❑ Herbal Tea
- ❑ Coffee
- ❑ Cocoa

Dairy
(<3g Fat/Serving)

- ❑ Freshly Grated Parmesan Cheese
- ❑ Low-fat Cheese
- ❑ Low-fat Cottage Cheese
- ❑ Non-fat Plain Yogurt
- ❑ Skim or 1% Milk
- ❑ Trans Fat Free/Non Hydrogenated Butter Substitute

Meat, Poultry, Fish & Eggs

- ❑ Center Cut Pork Chops
- ❑ Eggs
- ❑ Lean Red Meat
- ❑ Salmon
- ❑ Scallops
- ❑ Shrimp
- ❑ Skinless Chicken Breast
- ❑ Skinless Turkey Breast
- ❑ Tilapia
- ❑ Tuna

Cereal, Grains & Bread
(3g+ Fiber & 3g Fat/Serving)

- ❑ Barley
- ❑ Brown & Wild Rice
- ❑ Bulgur
- ❑ Couscous
- ❑ Ground Flax Seed
- ❑ Oats
- ❑ Quinoa
- ❑ Unsweetened Cereal
- ❑ Wheat Germ
- ❑ Whole Grain Crackers
- ❑ Whole Grain Waffles
- ❑ Whole Wheat Bread
- ❑ Whole Wheat Pasta
- ❑ Whole Wheat Pita
- ❑ Whole Wheat Tortilla

Other Healthy Items

____

____

____

____

____

____

Dietitian
IN THE
KITCHEN

SOUPS

No matter what the season, there is a soup for you to enjoy, chilled soup for hot summer days and hot soup for cold winter nights. Most soups, whether from a can or ordered while dining out, contain much too much fat and sodium.

The great thing about homemade soups is that YOU control the ingredients. Pack them with healthy ingredients to create a powerhouse of nutrition in one large vessel! You can freeze this nutritious concoction in small containers for quick and healthy meals. So grab a stock pot and get started!

DIETITIAN in the KITCHEN™

RULE:

Use little or no salt in soup preparation and add it at the table if desired!

Autumn Soup

1 tablespoon olive oil
1 large sliced onion; sliced
1 celery stalk; coarsely chopped
1/4 teaspoon cinnamon
1 teaspoon ground ginger
1/4 teaspoon ground cumin
1/2 teaspoon dry mustard
1/2 teaspoon cayenne pepper
1/2 teaspoon garlic powder
Lots of freshly ground black pepper
2 cups peeled turnips; cubed
3 cups peeled butternut squash; cubed
3 cups peeled acorn squash; cubed
3 medium carrots; chopped
1 quart low-salt chicken or vegetable broth
2 cups 1% milk
Extra broth

1. Heat oil in a large stock pot over medium heat.
2. Add onion, celery and next 7 ingredients (cinnamon through black pepper); sauté 4 minutes.
3. Reduce heat to low; cover and cook 3 minutes.
4. Add turnips, squash, carrots, and broth.
5. Bring to a boil, reduce heat and simmer, partially covered for 30 minutes or until tender.
6. Place one-third of mixture into a blender or food processor and process until smooth.
7. Pour pureed mixture into a large bowl. Repeat step 6 with remaining mixture.
8. Return pureed mixture to pot and stir in milk.
9. Cook over low heat until thoroughly heated, stirring occasionally. Thin with extra broth if needed.
10. Enjoy!

Serves 6-8

Vegetable Bisque Soup

1 tablespoon olive oil
1 cup chopped onion
1 cup chopped celery
1 cup chopped carrot
3 cups low-sodium vegetable stock
3 medium tomatoes; peeled & coarsely chopped
1/2 cup fresh parsley
1/2 cup fresh basil leaves
1/2 teaspoon paprika
1 teaspoon garlic powder
1 cup 1% milk
1/4 cup fresh basil leaves, finely chopped
Salt & freshly ground black pepper to taste

1. Heat oil in large stockpot over medium heat.
2. Add onion, celery and carrot; sauté until slightly brown.
3. Add stock and next 5 ingredients (stock through garlic powder), bring to a boil.
4. Reduce heat and simmer about 20 minutes.
5. Cool the mixture slightly.
6. Place one-third of mixture into blender or food processor and process until smooth
7. Pour pureed mixture into large bowl. Repeat step 6 with remaining mixture.
8. Return pureed mixture to pot and stir in milk. Add additional milk as desired.
9. Cook over low heat until thoroughly heated, stirring occasionally.
10. Garnish with chopped basil
11. Enjoy!

Serves 6

Black-Bean Soup

1 tablespoon olive oil
3 cloves garlic; minced
1 cup onion; chopped
1 cup carrot; thinly sliced
1 teaspoon ground cumin
4 cups low-sodium chicken or vegetable stock
3 cups cooked black beans
2 teaspoon dried cilantro
1/4 teaspoon ground red pepper
Lots of freshly ground black pepper
1/2 cup low-fat sour cream
1/2 cup chopped fresh cilantro

1. In a large sauce pan, sauté garlic, onion and carrot in oil over medium heat for about 5 minutes.
2. Add next 5 ingredients (cumin through red pepper).
3. Cook over low heat for about 25 minutes.
4. Remove from heat and add pepper to taste.
5. Ladle into bowls and top with 1 tablespoon low-fat sour cream and 1 tablespoon cilantro.
6. Enjoy!

Serves 6-8

Clam Chowder

4 slices turkey bacon
1 large onion; sliced
1/2 cup celery; chopped
1/2 cup carrots; chopped
2 cups potatoes; peeled and diced
3 cups water
3 cups fresh or canned clams and liquid
1 tablespoon dried thyme
28 ounce can diced tomatoes
Freshly ground black pepper
1/4 cup chopped parsley
Few shakes of Tabasco sauce

1. Cook turkey bacon over low heat in a large pan for about 3 minutes. Remove from pan and crumble. Return turkey bacon to pan.
2. Add onion and celery and saute until golden.
3. Add carrots, potatoes, water and clams with liquid.
4. Simmer covered over low heat for about 30 minutes.
5. Add thyme, tomatoes, parsley and Tabasco and simmer about 10 minutes.
6. Season to taste with pepper.
7. Enjoy!

Serves 8-10

Gazpacho

3 cucumbers; peeled & coarsely chopped
2 large sweet red peppers, coarsely chopped
1 medium red onion, coarsely chopped
1 lb. plum tomatoes, cut in half
2 medium garlic cloves, minced
16 ounces low-sodium tomato juice
2 tablespoons red wine vinegar
2 tablespoons fresh lime juice
1 tablespoons cayenne pepper (optional)
1 cup parsley; finely chopped (reserve 2 tablespoons for garnish)
1/4 cup cilantro; finely chopped (reserve 2 tablespoons for garnish)
1/4 cup olive oil
Add 3/4 cup diced avocado

1. Pulse cucumber in food processor and place in large bowl.
2. Repeat with red pepper, onion and tomatoes.
3. Add next 8 ingredients to bowl (garlic through olive oil).
4. Stir very well and refrigerate for at least 30 minutes.
5. Just before serving, stir well and add salt and pepper to taste.
6. Serve in individual bowls and garnish with 1 tablespoon avocado and a sprinkle of parsley and cilantro.
7. Enjoy!

Serves 6-8

Dietitian
IN THE
KITCHEN

STARTERS

Starters, appetizers or first courses (whichever term you choose) can serve many functions; something to munch on while dinner is being prepared, an offering at a cocktail party or possibly a main course when accompanied with a salad. The following starters are light and uncomplicated yet loaded with nutritious ingredients. Present them on colorful plates and bowls and they are sure to impress!

DIETITIAN in the KITCHEN™

RULE:

Remember...starters should be consumed in small portions if a meal is to follow!

Fiery Chicken Bites

Fiery Marinade

2 tablespoons olive oil

3 tablespoons of hot sauce

1/4 cup water

1 tablespoon freshly squeezed lemon juice

1/2 cup rice wine vinegar

1. In medium saucepan heat hot sauce in olive oil for about 3 minutes.
2. Add remaining ingredients and simmer for about 10 minutes.
3. Let cool slightly.

1 lb. boneless chicken breasts; lightly pounded

1. Place chicken and 1 cup Fiery Marinade in zip lock bag and marinate for at least 3 hours....the longer the better!
2. Remove chicken from marinade and grill until done (about 5 minutes per side).
3. Pour some marinade on top before turning.
4. Remove from grill and chop into bite-sized pieces.
5. Serve with 2 tablespoons Creamy Dipping Sauce (page 96) and vegetable stalks.
6. Enjoy!

Serves 4-6

Stuffed Endive Leaves

- 16 endive leaves, washed
- 4 cups shiitake mushroom caps, finely chopped
- 1 cup cremini mushroom caps, finely chopped
- 1 cup oyster mushrooms, finely chopped
- 2 cups white mushroom caps, finely chopped
- 2 teaspoons olive oil
- 2 garlic cloves, minced
- 1/4 cup white wine
- 1/4 cup Marsala wine
- 2 teaspoons fresh thyme leaves, finely chopped
- 2 teaspoons fresh parsley, finely chopped
- 1 teaspoon cayenne pepper
- Lots of freshly ground pepper to taste

1. Arrange endive leaves on platter and chill in refrigerator.
2. Place mushrooms in food processor; pulse until finely chopped.
3. Heat olive oil in pan, add garlic and sauté 2 minutes.
4. Add mushrooms, white and marsala wine. Sauté 5-6 minutes or until most of liquid evaporates.
5. Add thyme, parsley, cayenne and pepper.
6. Cook 3 minutes, stirring occasionally.
7. Add more pepper to taste.
8. Spoon 1 tablespoon of mixture into each endive leave.
9. Serve immediately.
10. Enjoy!

Serves 8 *(2 endive leaves and 2 tablespoons mixture per person)*

Eggplant Caponata

2 tablespoons olive oil

1 small eggplant, coarsely chopped, unpeeled

Chicken or vegetable broth

1 medium yellow onion, peeled & minced

1/2 cup minced celery

1 cup tomato puree

1/2 cup coarsely chopped Kalamata olives

2 tablespoons anchovy paste

2 tablespoons capers

2 tablespoons red wine vinegar

Lots of freshly ground black pepper

1. Heat oil in a large, heavy saucepan 1 minute over high heat.
2. Add eggplant and sauté, stirring occasionally and adding broth to prevent sticking, about 10 minutes until nearly translucent.
3. Add onion and celery and cook 5 minutes.
4. Add remaining ingredients, cover, and simmer 1 & 1/2 hours until quite thick, stirring occasionally.
5. Remove from heat and mash with potato masher.
6. Cool to room temperature.
7. Taste and adjust pepper as needed.
8. Serve as a spread for crackers or crostini or as dip for raw veggies.
9. Enjoy!

Serves 10-12

Guacamole

1 Haas avocado
3 tablespoon chopped onion
1 & 1/4 teaspoon chopped cilantro
2 tablespoons chopped tomato (discard juice & seeds)
1 teaspoon jalapeno pepper, chopped
1/4 teaspoon kosher salt

1. Place 1 tablespoon chopped onion, 1/2 teaspoon chopped jalapeno and 1/2 chopped cilantro in food processor, blender or mortar and pestle to form a paste
2. Split the avocado in half lengthwise and remove seed. Slice in half lengthwise in 1/8 inch strips, then across to form a grid. Scoop it out of the skin with a spoon.
3. Add avocado to the paste and thoroughly mix together.
4. Add the remaining ingredients and fold.
5. Serve with freshly baked corn tortilla chips
6. Enjoy!

Serves 2

Fresh Tomato Salsa

4 medium tomatoes, cored, diced
1 medium cucumber; seeded, diced
1 teaspoon olive oil
2 minced garlic cloves
1/2 cup diced red onion
1/4 cup chopped cilantro
1 tablespoon fresh lime juice
2 teaspoons jalapeno pepper, chopped (optional)
1/4 teaspoon salt
1/4 teaspoon pepper

1. Combine all ingredients together.
2. Let stand at room temperature for 15 minutes to meld flavors.
3. Add salt and pepper to taste.
4. Chill until ready to serve.
5. Serve with freshly baked corn tortilla chips.
6. Enjoy!

Serves 4

Dietitian
IN THE
KITCHEN™

SALADS

I love salads! Not just because I am a Registered Dietitian but because they are so versatile. Salads can be served at the beginning or end of a meal and even function as the main meal when lean protein is added. Fruits, crunchy veggies, nuts and seeds in salads can be added for a range of textures. There is really no need to measure the amount of greens in these salads so use as much or as little as you like. It is the portion size of the dressing that adds the most calories. Substitute any fruits, nuts and added vegetables that you like. Dressings can be made 1 day ahead of time for added convenience. Enjoy this diverse selection of sensational salads!

DIETITIAN in the KITCHEN™

RULE:

Use half the dressing first and toss your salad.
Chances are you will not need to add any more.

Greek Salad

DRESSING:

1/4 cup olive oil

1 tablespoon red wine vinegar

2 tablespoons freshly squeezed lemon juice

1 clove garlic; minced

1 tablespoon dried oregano

Lots of freshly ground black pepper

SALAD:

4 cups chilled coarsely chopped romaine lettuce

1 cup cucumber; seeded & coarsely chopped

1/2 cup red onion; diced

1/4 cup Kalamata olives; pitted and chopped

1/2 cup fresh parsley; chopped

TOPPINGS:

1/4 cup feta cheese; crumbled

8 anchovy filets

1. Combine all ingredients for dressing in a bowl and whisk well. Set aside.
2. Place all ingredients for salad in a bowl.
3. Drizzle one half of dressing over salad and toss well.
7. Add remaining dressing if needed and feta and gently re-toss.
8. Top with anchovy filets and serve immediately.
9. Enjoy!

Fennel Walnut Salad

with White Balsamic Citrus Vinaigrette

DRESSING:

1/2 cup fresh squeezed orange juice

1 teaspoon fresh squeezed lemon juice

2 medium garlic cloves, minced

2 tablespoons fresh mint leaves, chopped

1 tablespoon white balsamic vinegar

1/4 cup water

1/2 cup olive oil

1/2 teaspoon freshly ground black pepper

SALAD:

5 cups mixed baby greens

1 & 1/2 cups shredded carrots

1 fennel bulb, white and very pale green parts only, washed and sliced thinly

TOPPINGS:

1 & 1/2 cup orange segments, coarsely chopped

1/2 cup crushed walnuts, toasted*

*To toast walnuts: Place in dry pan over medium heat until lightly brown and aroma is intensely nutty.

1. Combine all ingredients for dressing in a bowl whisk vigorously.
2. Place all ingredients for salad in large bowl and toss well.
3. Drizzle one half of dressing over salad and toss well.
4. Add remaining dressing if needed and re-toss.
5. Add oranges and walnuts, toss gently.
6. Enjoy!

Tossed Greens
with Strawberry Flax Vinaigrette

DRESSING:

1/2 cup olive oil

1 tablespoon red wine vinegar

1 teaspoon balsamic vinegar

2 cup whole strawberries; washed & cored

1/4 cup ground flax seeds

2 medium garlic cloves, minced

1 teaspoon freshly ground black pepper

Water as needed

SALAD:

1 head chilled romaine lettuce: chopped

5 cups mixed baby greens

1/2 head red cabbage; thinly sliced

1. Combine all ingredients for dressing in a blender and blend completely. Add water if too thick.
2. Place lettuce and cabbage in a large serving bowl.
3. Drizzle one half of dressing over salad and toss well.
4. Add remaining dressing if needed and re-toss.
5. Serve immediately.
6. Enjoy!

Carrot & Cabbage Salad

Dressing:

2 tablespoons red wine vinegar

1 tablespoon olive oil

1 tablespoons sugar

1 teaspoon dry mustard

2 tablespoons water

3 tablespoons fresh squeezed orange juice

2 teaspoon fresh parsley, chopped

Lots of freshly ground pepper

Salad:

2 cups thinly sliced red cabbage

2 cups thinly sliced green cabbage

2 cups grated carrot

1 small onion, thinly sliced

3/4 cup toasted slivered almonds*

*To toast almonds: Place in dry pan over medium heat until lightly brown and aroma is intensely nutty.

1. Combine first 8 ingredients together (vinegar through pepper) with wire whisk. Set aside.
2. Combine cabbage, carrot and onion together in large bowl.
3. Add vinegar mixture to cabbage mixture and toss well.
4. Add 1/2 cup almonds and re-toss.
5. Sprinkle with 1 tablespoon toasted almonds before serving.
6. Enjoy!

Watercress & Fruit Salad

DRESSING:

1/4 cup olive oil

1 tablespoon rice vinegar

1 teaspoon chopped fresh tarragon

2 tablespoon freshly squeezed orange juice

1 medium garlic clove, minced

Lots of freshly ground black pepper

SALAD:

2 bunches watercress; washed and most of stem cut off

1/2 cup fresh papaya; peeled, diced & seeded

1/2 cup apples; peeled and diced

1/4 cup dried cranberries

1. Combine all ingredients for dressing in a bowl and whisk vigorously.
2. Place all ingredients for salad in large bowl and toss gently.
3. Drizzle one half of dressing over salad and toss well.
4. Add remaining dressing if needed and re-toss.
5. Enjoy!

Kiwi & Pine Nut Salad

DRESSING:

1/4 cup fresh squeezed orange juice

2 medium garlic cloves, minced

2 tablespoons fresh basil leaves, chopped

1 tablespoon balsamic vinegar

1/2 cup olive oil

1/2 teaspoon freshly ground black pepper

SALAD:

5 cups mixed baby greens

1 & 1/2 cup thinly sliced red bell pepper

1 & 1/2 cup shredded carrots

TOPPINGS:

1 & 1/2 cup coarsely chopped kiwi

1/2 cup pine nuts, toasted*

*To toast pine nuts: Place in dry pan over medium heat until lightly brown and aroma is intensely nutty.

1. Combine all ingredients for dressing in a bowl whisk vigorously.
2. Place all ingredients for salad in large bowl and toss well.
3. Drizzle one half of dressing over salad and toss well.
7. Add remaining dressing if needed and re-toss.
8. Add kiwi and pine nuts; toss gently.
9. Enjoy!

Sensational Caesar Salad

DRESSING:

1/2 cup plain non-fat yogurt
1 teaspoon olive oil
Juice of 1/2 lemon
1 & 1/2 teaspoon red wine vinegar
1/2 teaspoon balsamic vinegar
1 tablespoon Worcestershire sauce
2 teaspoon Dijon mustard
1 tablespoon anchovy paste
2 medium garlic cloves, minced
1 teaspoon freshly ground black pepper

SALAD:

1 head chilled sliced romaine lettuce
1 tablespoon grated fresh parmesan cheese

CROUTONS:

5 cups multi-grain bread cubes (1/2 inch)
1/2 teaspoon garlic powder
Olive oil cooking spray (or equivalent imitation)

1. Preheat oven to 325°.
2. Place bread cubes in a bowl spray lightly with olive oil spray and toss. Repeat until bread is lightly coated.
3. Sprinkle one half garlic powder and toss. Add remaining powder and re-toss.
4. Place on a baking sheet. Bake for 15 minutes or until golden and crisp. Set croutons aside.
5. Combine all ingredients for dressing in a bowl and whisk well. Set aside
6. Place lettuce in a large serving bowl. Drizzle one half of dressing over salad and toss well.
7. Add remaining dressing if needed and parmesan cheese and re-toss.
8. Top with croutons and serve immediately.
9. Enjoy!

Spinach Salad

with Fresh Pear and Toasted Almonds

Dressing:

2 tablespoons ground flax seeds

1/4 cup peanut oil

1/4 cup olive oil

2 tablespoons red wine vinegar

1 tablespoon balsamic vinegar

Juice of 1 orange

1 medium garlic clove, minced

Lots of freshly ground black pepper

Salad:

5 cups baby spinach

1 cup mushrooms

1 & 1/2 cup shredded carrots

Toppings:

1 & 1/2 cup fresh pears, peeled & coarsely chopped

1/2 cup slivered almonds, toasted*

*To toast almonds: Place in dry pan over medium heat until lightly brown and aroma is intensely nutty.

1. Combine all ingredients for dressing in a bowl and whisk well.
2. Place ingredients for salad in large bowl and toss well.
3. Drizzle one half of dressing over salad and toss well.
7. Add remaining dressing if needed and re-toss.
8. Add pears and almonds, toss gently.
9. Enjoy!

Jicama & Orange Salad

Dressing:

1/2 cup fresh squeezed orange juice

1 teaspoon fresh squeezed lemon juice

2 medium garlic cloves, minced

2 tablespoons fresh mint leaves, chopped

1 tablespoon white balsamic vinegar

1/2 cup olive oil

Lots of freshly ground black pepper

Salad:

1 medium jicama bulb; peeled, cut in 2 inch batons

2 large cucumbers, peeled, cut in 2 inch batons

1 medium red onion, sliced

1 & 1/2 cup orange segments

1 jalapeno; ribs & seeds removed, finely chopped

1. Combine all ingredients for dressing in a bowl whisk vigorously.
2. Place all ingredients for salad in large bowl and toss well.
3. Drizzle one half of dressing over salad and toss well.
4. Add remaining dressing if needed and re-toss.
5. Enjoy!

Dietitian
IN THE
KITCHEN™

Entrées

When choosing the main protein of the entrée always consider the quantity and quality of the fat you will be consuming. Avoid saturated fats as often as possible as they have a negative effect on your heart. Saturated fat is found in products of animal origin and the concentration is higher when skin or visible fat is not removed. Choose skinless, boneless poultry and trim all visible fat from meats. Unsaturated fats are the heart-healthy fats of choice and are found in fish, shellfish and plant-based meals. For a change of pace try to have at least 1 meatless meal per week!

DIETITIAN in the KITCHEN™

RULE:

Consume lean red meat no more than once a week and have fish at least 2 times per week.

Baked Salmon Filet

with Cannellini Puree

1 (9 inch) salmon filet, skinned
Olive oil spray
1 teaspoon fresh lemon juice
1/4 cup drained capers
2 teaspoons freshly ground black pepper

Cannellini Puree
2 cups cooked cannellini beans
2 cloves fresh garlic
2 tablespoons fresh lemon juice
1/4 cup freshly chopped parsley
2 teaspoon freshly ground black pepper
Water

1. Preheat oven to 325°
2. Combine all ingredients for puree in blender. Blend until smooth; adding water as needed. Set aside.
3. Rinse salmon filet and pat dry with a paper towel.
4. Place salmon on bottom of large casserole dish sprayed lightly with olive oil spray.
5. Pour 1 teaspoon lemon juice over salmon and turn to moisten completely.
6. Spread puree on top of salmon with rubber spatula.
7. Sprinkle capers and pepper on top of puree evenly.
8. Bake covered for 15 minutes. Lightly baste with pan juices.
9. Continue baking 10 minutes or until salmon turns pale pink.
10. Enjoy!

Serves 4

Lemon Chicken

with Savory Dill Rub

Juice of 4 lemons
3 garlic cloves; minced
Lots of freshly ground black pepper
16 oz. chicken breasts; lightly pounded

RUB:

2 tablespoons minced fresh dill
1 tablespoon brown sugar
1 tablespoon minced onion
1 tablespoon minced garlic
1 teaspoon chili powder
1/4 teaspoon kosher salt
Lots of freshly ground black pepper
1/4 cup freshly squeezed orange juice
1/4 cup low-sodium chicken broth

1. Whisk lemon juice, garlic and pepper together in small bowl.
2. Place chicken and lemon juice mixture in large ziplock bag and marinate for at least 4 hours (the longer the better!).
3. Combine rub ingredients in small bowl. Set aside.
4. Remove chicken from lemon juice mixture and place on large platter.
5. Rub chicken completely cover and place back in refrigerator for at least 30 minutes.
6. Heat grill or pan on medium-high for 5 minutes.
7. Place chicken on grill or in pan; cook for 5 minutes. Turn and sear 5 more minutes or until done.
8. Remove from pan.
9. Quickly add broth and juice to pan and reduce slightly. Drizzle over chicken and serve immediately.
10. Enjoy!

Serves 4-5

Fig Basted Grilled Shrimp

1 lb. large shrimp; peeled & deveined with tails on

BASTING SAUCE:

3/4 cup fig preserves

1 tablespoon fresh lime juice

1 teaspoon chili paste

1 tablespoon rice vinegar

1/4 teaspoon salt

1/4 teaspoon pepper

1. Combine all ingredients for sauce in a small bowl with a whisk. Reserve 1/4 cup sauce.
2. Add shrimp; toss to coat. Cover bowl with plastic wrap and marinate maximum 20 minutes.
3. Heat grill or grill pan until medium-hot.
4. Thread shrimp on skewers; baste with marinade. (if using wooden skewers; soak for 30 minutes prior to using)
5. Grill until shrimp are pink and cooked through; turning once and basting again.
6. Place shrimp on serving plates and top with reserved sauce.
7. Enjoy!

Serves 4-5

Chicken & Barley

with Vegetable Medley

1 tablespoon olive oil
3/4 cup diced carrot
1 thyme sprig
3/4 cup diced celery
3/4 cup thinly sliced leek; pale green and white parts only
1/2 cup finely chopped onion
1/2 teaspoon salt & pepper
4 skinless, boneless chicken breasts, cut into 1/4 inch strips
1 & 3/4 cup uncooked pearl barley
6 cups chicken broth
1 cup water
1/2 cup chopped fresh flat-leaf parsley
1/2 cup grated fresh Parmesan cheese

1. Heat oil in a large pot over medium-high heat.
2. Add carrot and thyme; saute I minute.
3. Add celery, leek and onion; saute I minute.
4. Add salt, pepper and chicken; saute 5 minutes.
5. Add barley; saute I minute.
6. Add broth and water; bring to a boil.
7. Cover, reduce heat, and simmer 40 minutes.
8. Remove from heat; discard thyme sprig.
9. Stir in parsley and cheese.
10. Enjoy!

Serves 8

Tex-Mex Tofu Burritos

1 (10.5 oz.) package extra-firm tofu, drained, pressed, sliced in 1/2" x 3" strips

2 teaspoons Worcester sauce

2 teaspoons red wine vinegar

2 teaspoons steak sauce

1/2 teaspoon ground cumin

1/4 teaspoon garlic powder

1 teaspoon ground ginger

1/2 teaspoon chili powder

1/4 teaspoon salt

1/4 teaspoon pepper

4 (8 inch) chapatis (whole-wheat tortillas)

1 teaspoon Canola oil

1 cup red bell pepper strips

1 cup green bell pepper strips

1 cup sliced onion

1/4 cup chopped fresh cilantro leaves

2 cup mild salsa

1/4 cup reduced-fat shredded cheddar cheese

1/4 cup low-fat sour cream

1. Place tofu in a shallow dish.
2. Combine next 9 ingredients in a small bowl and whisk gently.
3. Pour mixture over tofu and toss gently to coat. Set aside.
4. Warm tortillas according to package directions.
5. Heat oil in large non-stick skillet over medium heat.
6. Add onion and peppers and sauté 6 minutes or until crisp-tender. Set aside, covered.
7. Heat heavy skillet sprayed with olive oil spray.
8. Pan sear tofu 2–4 minutes per side. Spray with oil as needed.
9. Gently mix in cilantro and 1cup salsa. Remove pan from heat. Keep warm.
10. Place 1 tablespoon cheese down the center of each chapati. Top with pepper and onion mixture, then tofu.
11. Roll chapatis to seam side down.
12. Top with 2 tablespoons salsa and 1tablespoon sour cream. Top with jalapeños to taste.
13. Enjoy!

Serves 4

Pan-Seared Scallops

with Sesame Seed Rub

20 sea scallops, rinsed & patted dry
3 tablespoons sesame seeds
2 tablespoons brown sugar
1 tablespoon dried, minced onion
1 tablespoon dried, minced garlic
1 teaspoon ground cumin
1 teaspoon chili powder
1/4 teaspoon kosher salt
Lots of freshly ground black pepper
2 tablespoons combo of roasted peanut & sesame oil
1/4 cup dry white wine
2 tablespoons light soy sauce
1/4 cup chicken broth
2 teaspoons arrowroot or cornstarch
1/4 cup combo chicken broth & white wine

1. Combine sesame seeds through black pepper in spice grinder and pulverize to soft powder.
2. Pour mixture onto platter in even layer.
3. Press scallops into mixture, turn over and repeat on other side. Set aside.
5. Heat 1 tablespoon oil in large cast iron pan or non-stick skillet over high heat.
6. Add scallops and pan sear 3-5 minutes per side. Add remaining oil as needed.
7. Reduce heat to medium, remove scallops, set aside and cover with foil.
8. Add white wine to skillet and scrape bottom if necessary. Add soy sauce and chicken broth.
9. Combine arrowroot and wine/broth mixture w/whisk.
10. Add to pan and mix well until slightly thickened. Thin with broth as needed.
11. Drizzle over scallops and serve immediately.
12. Enjoy!

Serves 4

Seafood Ragout

4 cups fresh tomato, coarsely chopped

3/4 cups leek, white & pale green parts only, thinly sliced

1/2 cup dry white wine

1 tablespoon balsamic vinegar

2 garlic cloves, minced

3 tablespoons capers, drained

2 tablespoons fresh lemon juice

1 tablespoon hot cherry pepper, minced

1/2 cup sweet corn kernels

2 tablespoons fresh thyme leaves

1 tablespoon olive oil

1/2 pound shrimp

1/2 pound sea scallops

1/2 pound tuna steak, cubed

1 & 1/2 cups chopped fresh clams

Vegetable or fish stock as needed

4 cups cooked brown rice

1/2 cup chopped fresh flat-leaf parsley

1. Combine first 10 ingredients in a large saucepan (tomato through thyme) and toss well to combine all flavors.
2. Turn heat to medium-low and simmer, stirring occasionally.
3. Heat oil in large pan, add shrimp sauté 1 minute.
4. Add scallops, tuna and clams, toss gently for 2 minutes.
5. Add tomato mixture to seafood and toss gently to combine.
6. Add stock as needed.
7. Place 1/4 cup cooked rice into individual serving bowls.
8. Ladle the ragout into bowls and serve sprinkled with parsley.
9. Enjoy!

Serves 8

Chicken Murphy
with Turkey Sausage

1 tablespoon olive oil
4 links turkey or chicken sausage
2 large cloves garlic; minced
1 lb. skinless, boneless chicken breasts; lightly pounded
2 red bell peppers, sliced
2 medium onions; sliced
2 cups sliced mushrooms (white &/or wild)
3/4 cup thinly sliced sweet vinegar peppers
2 cups chicken or vegetable stock
Fresh oregano
Fresh rosemary
1/2 cup white wine
Few shots of light soy sauce
Freshly ground black pepper
Sliced hot cherry peppers (if desired)

1. Heat 1 teaspoon oil in a large pan over medium-high heat.
2. Brown sausage links and remove from pan.
3. Add 2 teaspoons oil to pan and add garlic; sauté 1 minute.
4. Add chicken; sauté 3-4 minutes per side until done and remove from pan.
5. Add bell peppers and onions to pan; sauté 5 minutes, stirring often.
6. Slice sausage in 1/2 inch rings and chicken into thin slices and add to pan.
7. Add mushrooms and vinegar peppers; sauté 1 minute.
8. Combine stock, oregano, rosemary and white wine and add to pan. Let mixture reduce slightly.
9. Add soy sauce and black pepper to taste.
10. Add hot cherry peppers if desired.
11. Enjoy!

Serves 6

Baked Salmon

with Ricotta and Parsley

1 (9 inch) salmon filet, skinned
Olive oil
1 teaspoon fresh lemon juice
1 cup chopped fresh parsley
2 teaspoon freshly ground black pepper

Ricotta Mixture:
16 oz. container part-skim ricotta
2 cloves fresh garlic; minced
2 tablespoons fresh lemon juice
1/2 cup freshly chopped parsley
2 teaspoons freshly ground black pepper

1. Preheat oven to 325°.
2. Combine all ingredients for ricotta mixture in large bowl. Mix until thoroughly combined. Set aside.
3. Rinse salmon filet and pat dry with a paper towel.
4. Place salmon on bottom of large casserole dish drizzled lightly with olive oil.
5. Pour 1 teaspoon lemon juice over salmon and turn to moisten completely.
6. Spread ricotta mixture on top of salmon with rubber spatula.
7. Sprinkle parsley on top of puree evenly.
8. Grind pepper over top.
9. Baked covered 15 minutes. Lightly baste with pan juices.
10. Continue baking 10 minutes or until salmon turns pale pink.
11. Enjoy!

Serves 6

Dietitian
IN THE
KITCHEN

VEGGIE
SIDES

Many of us are very comfortable using the same few vegetables at all meals.Time to experiment with some new varieties! Vegetables are chock full of nutrition, in particular, phytochemicals. Phytochemicals are plant based nutrients that have health promoting properties. They are also filled with fiber which is essential for good health. An important note is that the more color you have on your plate, the more nutrition. Vegetables can be prepared in many healthy ways; steamed, baked, broiled, roasted, braised and grilled. There is no need to prepare vegetables with excess fat. If you choose to cook your vegetables with olive oil - use a very small amount. Vegetables give off a lot of water so additional oil is unnecessary and will only add more calories.

DIETITIAN in the KITCHEN™

RULE:

For optimal nutrition, fill your dinner plate with 50% veggies!

Oven Baked Asparagus

1 lb fresh asparagus; cleaned & trimmed
1 tablespoon rice vinegar
2 teaspoon dried thyme leaves
1 tablespoon white wine
1 tablespoon olive oil
1 teaspoon kosher salt
Freshly ground black pepper; to taste

1. Preheat oven to 350°.
2. Place asparagus in a large ziplock bag.
3. Combine vinegar, thyme, wine and oil in bowl and whisk thoroughly.
4. Pour into bag with asparagus and let marinade for at least 15 minutes.
5. Remove asparagus from bag and place in an even layer on baking sheet(s).
6. Bake 10 minutes until crisp/tender; shaking pan halfway through.
7. Remove from oven, sprinkle kosher salt and pepper to taste.
8. Serve immediately.
9. Enjoy!

Serves 4

Pineapple - Mango Salsa

1/2 medium pineapple, peeled, cored & diced (1 & 1/2 cup)
1 firm, ripe mango, diced
1 small jicama bulb; peeled and diced
1/2 cup diced red onion
2 medium tomatoes, cored, diced
1 tablespoon olive oil
2 minced garlic cloves
1/2 cup chopped cilantro
2 tablespoon fresh lime juice
2 teaspoon jalapeno pepper, chopped (optional)
Lots of freshly ground black pepper

1. Combine all ingredients together.
2. Let stand at room temperature for 15 minutes to meld flavors.
3. Add pepper to taste.
4. Chill until ready to serve.
5. Enjoy!

Serves 4

Braised Escarole

with Garlic and Lemon

1 head escarole; cleaned thoroughly
1 tablespoon olive oil
3 cloves garlic, minced
2 tablespoons white wine
1 tablespoon fresh lemon juice
2 tablespoons chopped fresh oregano
Salt & freshly ground black pepper; to taste

1. Bring large pot of water to a boil.
2. Prepare ice bath in large bowl.
3. Coarsely chop escarole place in boiling water for about 1 minute.
4. Drain and set immediately in ice bath to halt the cooking process.
5. Set aside to drain.
6. Heat oil in a large pan over medium-high heat.
7. Add garlic; sauté 1-2 minutes.
8. Add escarole and toss into garlic. Turn the heat to medium-low and add wine and lemon juice.
9. Add oregano; stir for 1 minute.

7\. Add salt and pepper.

8\. Serve hot or warm.

9\. Enjoy!

Serves 3-4

Oven Roasted Beets
and Pearl Onions

1/2 lb. medium beets; peeled & quartered
1/2 lb. pound pearl onions, peeled
2 tablespoons olive oil
1 tablespoon white balsamic vinegar
1 tablespoon ground rosemary
1 teaspoon cayenne pepper
1 tablespoon garlic powder
Lots of freshly ground pepper
2 cups orange segments

1. Preheat oven to 375°.
2. Place beets and onions in large bowl.
3. Add olive oil and vinegar and toss gently.
4. Combine spices in small bowl, add to beets and toss gently.
5. Gently stir in orange segments.
6. Place in baking dish or foil pan.
7. Cover and bake 10 minutes.
8. Remove cover and bake additional 20-30 minutes, stirring occasionally until fork tender.
9. Enjoy!

Serves 6

Marinated Grilled Veggies

MARINADE:

6 ounces low-sodium tomato juice

2 tablespoons red wine vinegar

1 tablespoon balsamic vinegar

1 tablespoon Worcestershire sauce

1 tablespoon liquid smoke

2 tablespoons olive oil

3 medium garlic cloves, minced

2 tablespoons maple syrup

2 teaspoons Dijon mustard

1 tablespoon paprika

2 teaspoons freshly ground black pepper

VEGGIES:

3 medium zucchini, sliced lengthwise in 1/4 inch slices

4 plum tomatoes, cut in half, lengthwise

2 large sweet red peppers, sliced in 3/4 inch rings

1 medium red onion, sliced in 3/4 inch slices

1 medium eggplant, sliced in 1/2 inch rings

1. Combine all ingredients for marinade in a bowl and whisk well. Set aside.
2. Place veggies in large bowl and toss with 1/4 cup marinade to coat.
3. Grill zucchini and tomatoes 3 minutes on each side or until lightly golden and tender. Set aside.
4. Grill sweet peppers, onion and eggplant for 8-10 minutes or until crisp-tender, turning often.
5. Place all veggies in marinade and marinate minimum of 30 minutes.
6. Return all veggies to preheated grill to reheat. Reserve marinade.
7. Remove from heat and place on large serving platter.
8. Drizzle with some of reserved marinade and serve immediately.
9. Enjoy!

Serves 5

Hashed Brussels Sprouts

2 cups Brussels sprouts; cleaned
1 tablespoon olive oil
1 clove garlic, minced
2 tablespoon white wine
2 teaspoon fresh lemon juice
2 tablespoon chopped fresh oregano
Freshly ground black pepper; to taste

1. Cut Brussels sprouts in half vertically, then coarsely chop them.
2. Heat oil in a large pan over medium-high heat.
3. Add Brussels sprouts and garlic; sauté until sprouts begin to char; 1-2 minutes.
4. Turn the heat to medium-low, add wine and lemon juice. Partially cover.
5. Cook for 3 minutes.
6. Add oregano; stir for 1 minute.
7. Add pepper.
8. Enjoy!

Serves 2

Oven Roasted Carrots

6 medium carrots, cut diagonally into 1 inch thick slices
2 tablespoons olive oil
1 tablespoon dried tarragon
1 teaspoon dried thyme
1 tablespoon garlic powder
Lots of freshly ground pepper
Low-sodium broth

1. Preheat oven to 375°.
2. Place carrots in large bowl.
3. Add olive oil and spices and toss gently.
4. Place in baking dish.
5. Cover and bake 20 minutes; stirring occasionally.
6. Remove cover and bake additional 10-20 minutes stirring occasionally until tender and browned. Add a little broth if needed to prevent sticking.
7. Enjoy!

Serves 6

Broccoli & Wild Mushrooms

1 tablespoon olive oil
2 cloves garlic, minced
1 large onion, sliced thinly
2 thyme sprigs
2 tablespoons chopped fresh tarragon
3 cups broccoli; cleaned and coarsely chopped
2 tablespoons marsala cooking wine
2 cups shiitake mushroom caps, sliced
2 cups oyster mushrooms, sliced
2 cups cremino mushrooms, sliced
Low-sodium vegetable or chicken broth; as needed
Freshly ground black pepper; to taste

1. Heat oil in a large pan over medium-high heat.
2. Add garlic; sauté 1 minute.
3. Add onion, thyme and tarragon; sauté 1-2 minutes.
4. Add broccoli; sauté 5 minutes.
5. Add marsala; sauté 1 minute.
6. Add mushrooms; sauté 5 minutes. Adding broth as needed.
7. Remove from heat; discard thyme sprigs.
9. Top with black pepper.
10. Enjoy!

Serves 8

Green Beans & Carrots
with Citrus Drizzle

4 & 1/2 cups carrots, cut diagonally into 1 1/2 inch thick slices

1 pound green beans, trimmed, cut in half

1 tablespoons corn starch

2 & 1/2 teaspoons water

Lots of freshly ground pepper

2 tablespoons slivered almonds, toasted*

*To toast almonds: Place in dry pan over medium heat until lightly brown and aroma is intensely nutty.

Citrus Drizzle:

1 cup fresh squeezed orange juice

1/2 tablespoon fresh squeezed lemon juice

1/2 tablespoon fresh squeezed lime juice

2 teaspoons orange zest

1 tablespoon olive oil

1 clove minced garlic

2 teaspoons freshly grated ginger

1/4 teaspoon pepper

1. Preheat oven to 375°.
2. Place carrots in boiling water for about 3 minutes. Drain and set aside.
3. Whisk ingredients for drizzle in bowl.
4. Toss carrots and green beans in 1 cup citrus mix.
5. Place in baking dish or foil pan (about 12" x 8" x 2").
6. Pour remaining mix on top of veggies.
7. Cover and bake 20-25 minutes, stirring occasionally, until tender.
8. Drain veggies in colander with bowl underneath to catch juices.
9. Transfer juices to small saucepan over low heat.
10. Place veggies in a serving bowl.
11. Mix cornstarch and water with wire whisk. Slowly add to reserved juices, whisking well.
12. Pour mixture on top of veggies and sprinkle with almonds.
13. Enjoy!

Serves 8-10

Dietitian
IN THE
KITCHEN

STARCHY
SIDES

So many people are afraid of starches due to the low carb/no carb craze. The truth is that whole grains and complex carbohydrates are good for you! The key is to consume them in the right portion sizes and avoid refined products. The refining process strips the grain of fiber, B vitamins, folate and many other healthful compounds. Whole grains and starchy vegetables have more calories than non-starchy veggies and lean proteins served in the same quantity.

DIETITIAN in the KITCHEN™

RULE:

Think. "1/2 cup cooked" as a serving size and healthy starches become an integral part of your healthy eating plan.

Sweet Potato Fries

2 medium sweet potatoes; peeled
2 tablespoons olive oil
2 teaspoon rice vinegar
2 tablespoons dried parsley
2 tablespoons ground rosemary
1/4 teaspoon salt
1/4 teaspoon freshly ground black pepper

1. Preheat oven to 350°.
2. Cut potatoes in 2 inch batons and place in large bowl.
3. Combine oil and vinegar. Add to sweet potatoes and toss gently.
4. Add parsley, rosemary, salt and pepper; toss again gently.
5. Place in even layer on baking sheet and bake until browned and crisp tender for 40 minutes.
   Shake pan halfway through baking… (approx. 20minimum)
6. Enjoy!

Corn Salad

2 cloves minced garlic
1/2 cup diced onion
1/2 cup diced red bell pepper
1 tablespoon olive oil
2 cups cooked corn
1 tablespoon Dijon mustard
Few shots of soy sauce
1 tablespoon water
Lots of freshly ground black pepper
1/4 diced jicama
1/4 seeded, diced cucumber

1. In medium saucepan, saute garlic, onions and red bell pepper in olive oil.
2. Add corn and combine gently.
3. Combine mustard, soy sauce, water and pepper together in small bowl and whisk. Set aside.
5. Add jicama and cucumber to corn mixture and stir gently.
6. Add dijon mixture and combine gently.
7. Season to taste with extra pepper.
8. Enjoy!

Multi-grain Pilaf

1 cup whole grain (brown rice, kashi, barley, etc)

Low-salt vegetable broth

1 teaspoon olive oil

1 medium cloves garlic, minced

1/4 cup chopped onion

1 cup grated carrot

1/2 teaspoon ground cinnamon

1/4 cup fresh chopped parsley

1/4 cup chopped dried apricots

1/4 cup chopped dried cranberries

1 tablespoon chopped, shelled, unsalted almonds, toasted

1 tablespoon chopped unsalted cashews, toasted*

Lots of freshly ground black pepper

*To toast cashews: Place in dry pan over medium heat until lightly brown and aroma is intensely nutty.

1. In large saucepan, bring grain, broth and water to a boil over high heat. (substitute 50% of water called for package on directions with broth)
2. Cook as directed on package until all liquid is absorbed.
3. When finished, stir thoroughly; add extra stock if needed. Cover and set aside.
4. Heat oil in large non-stick skillet over medium heat.
5. Add garlic and onion and sauté 1 minute. Add carrot, cinnamon and parsley; sauté 3 minutes.
6. Add apricots and cranberries; sauté 3 minutes.
7. Remove pan from heat.
8. Add pan mixture to cooked whole grain. Combine thoroughly.
9. Stir in toasted nuts and add pepper to taste.
10. Enjoy!

White Bean Salsa
in Raddichio Cups

1 head of radicchio
4 cups cooked cannellini beans
2 cups cucumber; peeled & finely chopped
1 cup diced red onion
2 medium tomatoes, cored, diced
1 tablespoon olive oil
2 minced garlic cloves
1/2 cup chopped cilantro
2 tablespoon fresh lime juice
2 teaspoon jalapeno pepper, chopped (optional)
Lots of freshly ground black pepper

1. Peel radicchio, wash leaves and chill until ready to use.
2. Combine remaining ingredients together.
3. Let stand at room temperature for 15 minutes to meld flavors.
4. Add pepper to taste.
5. Chill until ready to serve.
6. Serve 1 cup into each radicchio leaf.
7. Enjoy!

Parmesan Baked Polenta
and Broccoli Rabe

- 2 heads of broccoli rabe; cleaned, stem ends removed & coarsely chopped
- 2 teaspoons olive oil
- 2 cloves garlic; minced
- 2 tablespoons fresh lemon juice
- 1 teaspoon cayenne pepper
- Olive oil spray
- 2 cups instant polenta
- 2 liters water
- 1 cup grated parmesan cheese

1. Preheat oven to 325°.
2. Blanch broccoli rabe in large pot of boiling water for 2-3 minutes. Drain and set aside.
3. Heat olive oil over medium heat.
4. Add garlic and saute 1 minute.
5. Add lemon juice and cayenne.
6. Add broccoli rabe and toss gently.
7. Cook over medium heat for -2 minutes.
8. Reserve cooking liquid and set aside.
9. Cook polenta according to package directions.
10. Spray bottom of large casserole dish with olive oil spray. Layer dish with polenta, 1/3 cheese and broccoli rabe. Repeat layering.
11. Drizzle liquid from broccoli rabe and last 1/3 cheese.
12. Baked covered until heated thoroughly about 15 minutes.
13. Enjoy!

Toasted Bulgur Pilaf

1 cup Bulgur
1 cup low-salt vegetable or chicken broth
1/2 cup water
1 whole cinnamon stick
1 teaspoon dried parsley
1 Tablespoon chopped, shelled almonds, toasted
Salt & pepper to taste

1. Heat large skillet over medium-high heat. Add bulgur and toast 4-5 minutes.
2. In medium saucepan stir together bulgur, stock, water, cinnamon and parsley. Bring to a boil.
3. Cover and reduce heat to low. Simmer until all liquid is absorbed, about 15 minutes.
4. Discard cinnamon stick.
5. Stir in toasted almonds.
6. Add salt and pepper to taste.
7. Enjoy!

Whole Wheat Pasta Salad

1 tablespoon olive oil
2 garlic cloves; minced
1/4 cup sliced red onion
2 cups asparagus spears; cut in 1/3rds
1/2 cup mushrooms (any type); coarsely chopped
4 cups cooked whole wheat pasta
1/2 cup carrots; peeled & grated
1/2 cup chopped fresh tomatoes
1/4 cup black olives; sliced
1/4 cup chopped fresh parsley or basil
1/4 cup toasted pignoli nuts
2 tablespoon grated romano or parmesan cheese

1. Saute garlic and red onion in olive oil until onions are soft – about 5 minutes.
2. Add asparagus spears and mushrooms and saute for 3-4 minutes and remove from heat.
3. Add mixture to cooked pasta and stir gently.
4. Add carrots, tomatoes and olives and combine gently.
5. Serve on individual plates with a sprinkle of herbs, nuts, grated cheese and black pepper.
6. Enjoy!

Roasted Potato Wedges

2 Tablespoons olive oil
1 teaspoon red chili powder
1 teaspoon garlic powder
1 teaspoon dry mustard
1 teaspoon dried mixed herbs (any combination you like)
4 medium baking potatoes
Lots of freshly ground black pepper

1. Preheat oven to 400°.
2. Combine oil, chile powder, garlic powder, dry mustard and herbs in bowl. Whisk well.
3. Cut potatoes in half lengthwise and then into long wedges.
4. Toss potatoes with oil mixture
5. Place in even layer in roasting pan and bake until golden brown - about 20 minutes.
6. Season to taste with pepper.
7. Enjoy!

Oriental Brown & Wild Rice

1 cup combo of uncooked brown & wild rice
1 cup water
1 cup low-sodium chicken or vegetable broth
2 tablespoons rice vinegar
1 teaspoon sesame oil
1 teaspoon honey
2 teaspoons natural peanut butter
1/4 teaspoon ground red pepper
1/2 cup grated carrots
1 cup snow peas; washed and cut in 1/3rds
1/4 cup crushed unsalted peanuts

1. Rinse rice and place in pot with water and broth, cover and simmer for 45 minutes until water is absorbed and rice is tender.
2. Remove from heat and set aside.
3. Combine vinegar, oil, honey, peanut butter and red pepper in bowl and whisk well.
4. Transfer rice to a bowl and stir in carrots and snow peas.
5. Add dressing and combine thoroughly.
6. Cover and chill for minimum of 1 hour…the longer the better.
7. Toss in peanuts just before serving.
8. Enjoy!

Dietitian
IN THE
KITCHEN™

Dips & Sauces

Dips and sauces are a wonderful complement for lean proteins, fruits and vegetables. A flavorful sauce can transform an ordinary grilled chicken breast into a palate pleasing delight. An assortment of vegetables presented with savory dips are a refreshingly healthy appetizer. Don't hesitate to alternate the quantity and selection of herbs and spices to your liking. These flavorful dips and sauces may entice even the pickiest eater to grab a new vegetable and go for it!

DIETITIAN in the KITCHEN™

RULE:

Dunk! Don't scoop into dips.
You will consume less calories.

Creamy Dipping Sauce

1/2 cup reduced fat sour cream
1/4 cup reduced fat mayonnaise
1/4 cup blue cheese (about 2 ounces)
1 tablespoon freshly squeezed lemon juice
Lots of freshly ground black pepper
2 teaspoons dried dill
2 teaspoons dried chives
2 teaspoons dried basil
1 teaspoon garlic powder

1. Combine all ingredients together until fluffy. Store in refrigerator.
2. Enjoy!

Serving Size 1/4 cup

Horseradish - Dill Sauce

2 cups plain, non-fat yogurt
1 tablespoon fresh lemon juice
1 tablespoon white wine
1/2 cup fresh dill, finely chopped
2 tablespoons horseradish
Pinch of kosher salt
Lots of freshly ground black pepper

1. Combine all ingredients in bowl and whisk thoroughly.
2. Use as dip for raw veggies or as an accompaniment to lean poultry or fish.
3. Enjoy!

Serving Size 1/4 cup

Peach Basting Sauce

1 cup ripe, fresh peaches; coarsely chopped
1 tablespoon olive oil
2 tablespoons Worcester sauce
1/4 cup red wine vinegar
1 teaspoon minced garlic
1/2 teaspoon pepper

1. Combine all ingredients in blender until smooth.
2. Pour into small saucepan and bring to a boil. Remove from heat and cool 10 minutes, stirring occasionally.
3. Brush on fish, shellfish, lean meat, poultry or veggies during cooking.
4. Boil remaining sauce for 2 minutes and serve with cooked meal.
5. Enjoy!

Serving Size 1/4 cup

with Roasted Pepper and Garlic

1/4 cup olive oil
2 cups chick peas; cooked
2 tablespoon tahini paste
Juice of 1 lemon
1 garlic clove, coarsely chopped
1/2 large red pepper, roasted
1/2 cup Kalamata olives, pitted & finely chopped
Salt & freshly ground black pepper to taste
Assorted fresh veggies, cut into finger size pieces

1. Combine first 6 ingredients (olive oil thru red pepper) in food processor or blender and mix until smooth.
2. Transfer hummus into a large bowl and stir in olives.
3. Add salt and pepper to taste.
4. Spoon hummus into serving bowl and place on large serving plate.
5. Surround hummus with fresh veggies.
6. Enjoy!

Serving Size 1/4 cup hummus and lots of veggies

Mexicali Dip

1/2 cup plain non-fat yogurt
1/2 cup low-fat or non-fat mayo
1 tablespoon fresh lime juice
1 clove garlic, minced
2 tablespoon fresh cilantro, chopped
1/2 teaspoon cayenne pepper
1/4 teaspoon salt
1/4 teaspoon pepper

1. Combine all ingredients for dip together with a wire whisk.
2. Enjoy!

Serving Size 1/4 cup

Dietitian
IN THE
KITCHEN™

MARINADES

Marinades infuse flavor into foods before cooking. This liquid combination should have an acidic ingredient like vinegar, citrus juice or wine that will function as a tenderizer. The addition of herbs and spices will enhance the flavor of the finished product. Be advised that delicate foods like shrimp and fish will become mushy if left in the marinade too long so limit their time to 20-30 minutes. Sturdier foods like chicken and steak can be left in longer without sacrificing consistency. The following marinades can double as dressings for salads and also spice up whole grain and vegetable dishes!

DIETITIAN in the KITCHEN™

RULE:

NEVER serve a marinade that has been in contact
with raw meat, fish or poultry.
Set a little bit aside before using as a marinade
and drizzle it on before serving!

Ginger-Soy Marinade

1/4 cup sesame oil
1/4 cup olive oil
2 tablespoons rice vinegar
1 tablespoon light soy sauce
1 tablespoon freshly squeezed orange juice
1 medium garlic clove, minced
1/4 cup freshly grated ginger
Lots of freshly ground black pepper

1. Combine all ingredients for marinade in bowl with wire whisk.
2. Enjoy!

Honey Mustard Marinade

1/2 cup olive oil
1 & 1/2 tablespoon Dijon mustard
2 teaspoons fresh lemon juice
1 tablespoon honey
2 teaspoon minced fresh dill weed
2 teaspoon minced fresh chives
Lots of freshly ground black pepper
Water

1. Combine all ingredients for marinade in bowl with wire whisk.
2. Thin with water if desired.
3. Enjoy!

Citrus Vinaigrette Marinade

1/2 cup fresh squeezed orange juice
1 teaspoon fresh squeezed lemon juice
2 medium garlic cloves, minced
2 tablespoons fresh mint leaves, chopped
1 tablespoon red wine vinegar
1/4 cup water
1/4 cup olive oil
1/2 teaspoon freshly ground black pepper

1. Combine all ingredients for marinade in a bowl and whisk well.
2. Enjoy!

Balsamic Marinade

2 tablespoons red wine vinegar
1 tablespoon balsamic vinegar
1 tablespoon Worcestershire sauce
1/4 cup olive oil
1 tablespoon garlic powder
1 tablespoon dried basil
1 tablespoon dried oregano
1 tablespoon maple syrup
1 tablespoon paprika
Lots of freshly ground black pepper

1. Combine all ingredients for marinade in bowl and whisk well.
2. Enjoy!

Southwestern Marinade

2 tablespoons freshly squeezed lime juice
1 tablespoon Dijon mustard
1/4 cup olive oil
1/2 teaspoon chili powder
1/4 teaspoon cumin
1 teaspoon dried cilantro
Zest of 1 lime
1 tablespoon garlic powder, minced
Lots of freshly ground black pepper

1. Combine all ingredients for marinade in bowl and whisk well.
2. Enjoy!

Dietitian
IN THE
KITCHEN™

Sweet
Endings

Creating healthy and palatable desserts has taken a bit of trial and error but was well worth it. These indulgences have less fat, sugar and calories than most desserts but are not short on taste. While treating yourself to decadently delicious flavor you will be receiving an abundance of vitamins, minerals, fiber and phytochemicals. How wonderful is it to "have your cake and eat it too"?

DIETITIAN in the KITCHEN™

RULE:

If you are offered a tempting dessert that you know is not the best choice - taste it or share it. Do not deprive yourself!

Baked Fruit

with Frozen Yogurt

FILLING:

3 cups thinly sliced apples

1 mango - scored & separated

1/2 cup sliced strawberries

1/2 cup blueberries

1/2 cup diced pineapple (fresh or frozen)

2 teaspoons fresh lemon juice

TOPPING:

3 tablespoons all-purpose flour

1 tablespoon brown sugar

1/2 cup quick cooking oats

1/2 teaspoon ground cinnamon

1/4 teaspoon ground nutmeg

1/4 teaspoon ground ginger

2 tablespoons butter

2 cups Low-fat vanilla frozen yogurt

3 tablespoons pure maple syrup

1. Preheat oven to 425°.
2. Combine fruit (you can use any of your favorite fruits) and lemon juice together. Spoon half of mixture in to 8" x 8" x 2" metal or foil pan.
3. In separate bowl combine flour, brown sugar, oats, cinnamon, nutmeg and ginger. Stir well.
4. Cut in butter with pastry blender until mixture resembles coarse crumbs.
5. Sprinkle half of mixture evenly over fruit mixture. Add remaining fruit and sprinkle other half of mixture on top.
6. Cover pan tightly with foil.
7. Bake about 45 minutes.
8. Remove cover and bake additional 20 minutes.
9. Spoon approx. 1 cup fruit into small bowl.
10. Top with 1/4 cup yogurt and drizzle 1 teaspoon syrup on top.
11. Enjoy!

Poached Pears

with Spiced Port Wine

4 large Bosc pears
1/2 cup water
1 & 1/2 cup Port wine
1 tablespoon fresh lemon juice
1 teaspoon cinnamon
1 teaspoon ground ginger
1 teaspoon nutmeg
4 tablespoon crushed unsalted peanuts

1. Peel and core pears, leaving stems intact. Slice a 1/4 inch from base of each pear so it will sit flat.
2. Combine water, wine, lemon and spices in large saucepan. Bring to a boil.
3. Add pears; cover, reduce heat, and simmer 10 minutes or until tender.
4. Remove pears from cooking liquid using a slotted spoon. Set aside.
5. Bring cooking liquid to a boil. Boil 5 minutes.
6. Place pears in each of 4 bowls. Pour cooking liquid over pears.
7. Sprinkle each with 1 tablespoon peanuts.
8. Enjoy!

Serves 4

Brown Rice Pudding

2 cups cooked brown rice
3/4 cup 1% milk
1/4 cup light brown sugar
1 tablespoon butter; melted
1 teaspoon ground cinnamon
1 tablespoon toasted wheat germ

1. Preheat oven to 375°.
2. Combine first 6 ingredients (rice through cinnamon) in a bowl and stir well.
3. Transfer mixture to 8 inch baking pan.
4. Sprinkle with wheat germ, cover with foil.
5. Bake 30 minutes.
6. Serve warm or at room temperature.
7. Enjoy!

Serves 4-6

Bean Spice Bars

non-stick cooking spray
2 cups cooked chick peas
3/4 cup natural applesauce
1 whole egg plus 2 egg whites
1 cup mashed potatoes
1 teaspoon vanilla extract
1 & 1/2 cup rolled oats
1 & 1/4 cup light brown sugar
1 cup all-purpose flour
1 teaspoon ground cinnamon
1 teaspoon ground nutmeg
1 teaspoon baking soda
1 tablespoon toasted wheat germ
1 tablespoon sesame seeds, toasted
1/4 cup sunflower seeds

1. Preheat oven to 350°.
2. Spray a 8" x 11" baking pan with cooking spray.
3. Puree beans and applesauce in food processor on low.
4. Combine eggs, potatoes, and vanilla in a large bowl; mix until well blended. Add bean mixture.
5. Combine next 6 ingredients (oats through baking soda).
6. Add to potato mixture and mix well.
7. Stir in wheat germ, sunflower seeds and sesame seeds.
8. Transfer mixture to baking pan. Bake 30 minutes.
9. Cut into 20 pieces.
10. Enjoy!

Serving Size: 1 bar

Piña Colada Sundae

1 ripe pineapple; cut into 1 inch rings
2 cups low-fat frozen vanilla yogurt
1 lime cut in 4 segments
1/4 cup shredded coconut; toasted
1/4 cup slivered almonds; toasted
8 fresh cherries; pitted
1/4 cup light whipped cream
1 & 1/2 tablespoon Meyer's rum (optional)

1. Grill pineapple rings over medium heat until lightly browned on each side; about 4 minutes per side.
2. Remove from heat, coarsely chop and keep warm.
3. In a small dessert dish assemble sundae as follows:

    1/2 cup yogurt

    Juice of 1/4 lime

    1/4 cup grilled pineapple

    1 tablespoon almonds

    1 tablespoon whipped cream

    2 cherries

    1 tablespoon coconut

    Drizzle with rum (optional)

4. Enjoy!

Serves 4

Balsamic Fruit

with Ricotta Cream

- 3 cups strawberries; stemmed & sliced
- 1 & 1/2 cups blueberries
- 3 kiwi; peeled, quartered & cut in 8 chunks
- 1/2 cup balsamic vinegar
- 2 tablespoons freshly squeezed lemon juice
- 1 tablespoon granulated sugar
- 1/2 cup part-skim ricotta cheese
- 2 tablespoons evaporated skim milk
- 1/4 cup low-fat vanilla yogurt
- Pinch of cinnamon
- 1/2 cup toasted slivered almonds
- 1/2 cup toasted coconut

1. Place berries and kiwi in large dish.
2. Heat balsamic vinegar, lemon juice and sugar together for 2 minutes.
3. Remove from heat and pour over berries and kiwi; set aside. Refrigerate and let marinate at least 1 hour…the longer the better!
4. Whip together ricotta cheese and evaporated skim milk.
5. Gently fold in yogurt and cinnamon.
6. Place 1/4 cup fruit in bottom of dessert glass-top with 1 tablespoon ricotta mixture, 1/2 teaspoon almonds and 1/2 teaspoon toasted coconut - repeat 1 more time.
7. Enjoy!

Serves 6-8

Nut Crusted Frozen Yogurt

with Warm Citrus Topping

2 cups low-fat vanilla frozen yogurt
1 cup combo of almonds & pecans, toasted
2 teaspoons cinnamon
2 teaspoons ground dried ginger
2 teaspoons ground nutmeg
1 orange
1 pink grapefruit
Zests of 1 orange & 1 grapefruit
1/4 cup granulated sugar
1 teaspoon pure vanilla extract
Fresh mint leaves for garnish

1. Scoop frozen yogurt into 1/2 cup balls and place, covered in single layer in freezer.
2. Place toasted nuts in food processor, coffee grinder or blender and pulverize to soft powder.
3. Add spices to nuts and set aside.
4. Cut peel from citrus fruits being careful to not cut too much flesh away.
5. Cut segments from membranes, coarsely chop and set aside.
6. Squeeze juice from membranes into small bowl.
7. Combine zests, sugar and 1/4 cup water to boil, stirring until sugar is dissolved.
8. Reduce heat to low, add citrus segments and vanilla and cook about 2 minutes. Let cool slightly.
9. Place nut mixture in even layer on plate.
10. Roll ball of yogurt in mixture until lightly coated.
11. Repeat with remaining frozen yogurt balls.
12. Place each ball in small bowl and top with 2 tablespoon warm citrus topping.
13. Garnish with mint leaves and serve immediately.
14. Enjoy!

Serves 4

Glazed Roasted Bananas

1/4 cup light brown sugar
1/4 cup fresh lemon juice
2 tablespoons butter
1/4 teaspoon ground cinnamon
1/4 teaspoon dried ginger
1/4 teaspoon nutmeg

4 large firm ripe bananas
Cooking spray
1/2 cup chopped almonds, toasted
1/2 cup coconut, shredded & toasted
2 cups vanilla low-fat frozen yogurt

1. Preheat oven to 450°.
2. Combine first 4 ingredients in a bowl and set aside.
3. Cut bananas in half lengthwise.
4. Place banana halves, cut side up, on a pan coated with cooking spray.
5. Bake at 450° for 4 minutes.
6. Drizzle sugar mixture evenly over banana halves, and sprinkle with toasted almonds and coconut.
7. Bake an additional 3 minutes.
8. Cut each banana piece into thirds crosswise.
9. Serve bananas with frozen yogurt; drizzled with any remaining sugar mixture.
10. Enjoy!

Serves 8 *(1/2 banana and 1/4 cup frozen yogurt per person)*

Peach-Banana Smoothie

3/4 cup soft tofu
1/2 cup 1% milk (or soy milk)
1/2 cup plain non-fat yogurt
1/2 teaspoon vanilla extract
1 banana
1 fresh peach or 1/2 cup canned peaches; drained
1 teaspoon toasted wheat germ
1 teaspoon ground flax seed

1. Combine all ingredients together in blender until smooth.
2. Enjoy!

Serving Size: 1 cup

Note: You may substitute any fruit you like for the banana and peach. Experiment with quantity of ingredients to satisfy your taste. Increase yogurt to 1 & 1/4 cup if you do not choose to use tofu.

Dietitian
IN THE
KITCHEN™

NOTES